101 Marathon Tips

Run Your Best Marathon And Conquer Your Running Fears

Gemma Dobson

Podium Addict Coaching

Stream Fitness

101 Marathon Tips
Run Your Best Marathon
And Conquer Your Running Fears

Copyright © 2020 Gemma Dobson

All rights reserved. This book or any portion thereof may not be reproduced or used in any manner whatsoever without the express written permission of the author except for the use of brief quotations in a book review or scholarly journal.

Disclaimer

Prior to beginning any running training program, you must consult your GP, you should also consult your GP if you are substantially increasing your training load or intensity. Any application of the material in the book is at the sole risk of the reader and at the readers' discretion.

Responsibility for any injuries or any other negative effects resulting from the application of any of the information provided within this book is expressly disclaimed.

First Printing: April 2020

ISBN:

Publisher: Gemma Dobson, Stream Fitness and Podium Addict Coaching

www.streamfitness.co.uk

www.podiumaddict.com

Table of Contents

Introduction 1
Foreword 2
TRAINING AND PREPARATION 5
   1. Choose your Marathon Wisely 5
   2. Get a Running Watch 6
   3. Join a running club 6
   4. Get a Health Check 7
   5. Follow a Plan 7
   6. Get a Coach 8
   7. Be Consistent 10
   8. Adapt Your Plan 11
   9. Train in Bad Weather 12
  10. Join Strava 13
  11. Join Social Media 14
  12. Train Without Music 15
  13. Warm-up 15
  14. Always Cooldown 16
  15. Train at Your Race Start Time 17
  16. Train on Your Race Terrain 18
  17. Run Off-Road 19
  18. Cross-train 20
  19. Routine 20
  20. Learn to Pace Accurately 21
  21. Understand the Importance of SLOW 22
  22. Slow = Slow 26
  23. Podcasts Help 27

24. Celebrate Successes 27
25. Add Speedwork 28
26. Practice Race Nutrition 28
27. Do Strength Training 30
28. Stretch 30
29. Foam Roll 32
30. Respect the Taper 32
31. Do Yoga 34
32. Do a Half-Marathon Race 35
33. Include Running Drills 36
34. Don't Change Your Running Style. 37
35. Ask for Help 38
36. Balance Training with Life 39
37. Go to Parkrun 39
38. Prepare Mentally 40
39. Believe 42
40. Remind yourself of 'Why' 43
41. Write Down your Marathon Concerns 43
42. Let Missed Sessions Go 44
43. Avoid Panic Training 45
44. Don't Try Anything Funky in the Final Few Weeks 46
45. Avoid Negative People 47
46. Stitch 47
47. Embrace the Tiredness 48
48. The Hardest Part Of The Marathon Is The Training 49
49. Change The Subject 50

RECOVERY 51

50. Learn to Rest 51
51. If You Are Ill, Rest. 52
52. Respect Injuries 53

- 53. Get a Sports Massage 54
- 54. Refuel ASAP 55

KIT 57

- 55. Have At Least Two Pairs Of Running Trainers 57
- 56. Get A Running Gait Analysis 58
- 57. Socks 59
- 58. Support – Sports Bras and Boxers 59
- 59. Wear Less 60
- 60. Be Weatherproof 61
- 61. Chafing 62
- 62. Be Aero 63
- 63. Dress Rehearsal 64
- 64. Let Them Shout Your Name 65

NUTRITION 67

- 65. Count Race Day Calories 67
- 66. Eat More 68
- 67. Eat breakfast 69
- 68. Prepare to Feel Hungry 69
- 69. Hydrate Properly 70
- 70. Drink on The Move 72
- 71. Fuel Properly 72
- 72. Reduce Alcohol 73

THE RACE 75

- 73. Check the Weather 75
- 74. Read the Race Pack 75
- 75. Learn the Course 77
- 76. Plan your Pre-Race Travel 78
- 77. Plan your Race Day 79
- 78. Plan How You're Getting Home 79
- 79. Focus on The Finish 80

80. Complete the Emergency Information 81
81. Have a Bin Liner for the Start 81
82. Take Loo Roll 82
83. Negative Split 83
84. Run Consistently 84
85. Fuel and Hydrate Immediately 85
86. Sing 86
87. Talk to yourself! 87
88. Walk If You Need To 87
89. Smile! 88
90. Take Less 88
91. Beware, Sunburn 89
92. Absorb The Atmosphere 90
93. Have a Plan-B 90
94. Count! 92
95. Arrange A Rendezvous 93
96. Grunt, Nod or Say 'Hi' 93
97. Speed Up Towards The Finish 94
98. Hands Off of Your Watch 95
99. Have A Finish Line Bag Prepared 96
100. Take Time Off 96

RACE REPORTS 97
101. What To Do When You Have Finished Your Marathon… 97

Introduction

Running a marathon is a lifetime achievement for many people, it is a true show of discipline, dedication to training, strength and endurance.

This book is designed to help you with your race planning, preparation and training and the key areas to think about before race day. It also delves into your race strategy and what to do on the big day!

These tips are relevant to both beginners and more experienced runners who are looking to improve their times, make their training more efficient and to execute a better run on race day.

Foreword

When I first began running, I struggled to get to the end of the street without needing to stop and take a rest. I would look on in amazement at the marathon runners and those completing Parkrun in under 20 minutes without even breaking a sweat. Running was an unknown world at that time. I refused to even entertain the idea of running a marathon, I couldn't understand how it was possible!

Fast forward 6 years and I have run more than 7 marathon distance events and raced 4 Ironman triathlons, competed for Great Britain in the Age Group Teams at Triathlon, Duathlon and Aquathlon (in addition to 100's of shorter distance races) and completely changed my outlook on running. I run Podium Addict Race Team with co-owner Sam Thompson, coaching a successful Swim/Bike/Run team of athletes ranging from first timers through to GB Age Group Athletes. It's a complete change from the girl that couldn't even run to the end of the street in 2012!

So, what changed? When I first started to run, I would try and go as hard and fast as I could and run for as long as I could. It felt horrible, I was always tired and I would always get injured. My speed increased in the first few months but then plateaued because I'd be injured or exhausted. It wasn't the right way to train. This is so common across all new runners, especially those aiming for their first marathon. I began to learn that running slowly was the secret to running fast and from then my whole experience changed. I was able to up my mileage, run faster, learn to breathe, fuel and recover better.

Running is a journey and I would like to share my experiences, mistakes and successful habits to help you with your running journey. This book is a collection of 101 tips to help you be successful in your next marathon, whether that's a stand-alone marathon, or the marathon at the end of an Ironman triathlon.

If you have any questions or would like to get in touch, then I would be pleased to hear from you through either of my Instagram channels; @gemsiem @podiumaddict or @streamfitnessuk

Gemma Dobson

Author

101 Marathon Tips

Run Your Best Marathon
And Conquer Your Running Fears

TRAINING AND PREPARATION

1. Choose your Marathon Wisely

There are hundreds of different marathon races across the world. Choose an event that suits you, things to consider are;

- Climate. Will you be doing most of your training in a wet and windy country? Consider how you will cope if you run a marathon in a hot, dry country?

- Terrain. Do you want a challenging, hilly marathon or a steady, flat course? Do you want to run off- or on-road?

- Support. Do you want lots of friends and family to support you? Are they likely to travel long distances to be there?

- Cost. Marathon entry fees range drastically in price. Don't forget to add in travel and accommodation expenses too.

- Date. Do you have long enough to train before the race?

- Your Calendar. Do you have any holidays or big events already scheduled which might distract you from your training?

2. Get a Running Watch

The optimum way to keep track of your pace is by having it on your wrist, glance at it regularly and make sure you're keeping to the set pace for that session. The more experienced you get, the fewer times you'll need to check your watch – you'll know what it feels like to run at a set pace.

Most running watches now will upload to Strava and other training platforms easily. You can also set them to alert you when you're running too slow or too fast. Newer ones will also give you a virtual partner. New Garmin's will set you a race pace plan taking into account the course.

3. Join a running club

If you feel like you're struggling with all of the 'alone time' during your training, then joining a running club could be the solution. Running with people will help motivate you, you'll make some fantastic friends and you'll put more effort into those interval sessions.

Just make sure you don't let pride get in the way on your long slow runs and stick to your own pace. Avoid getting sucked into running hard intervals on the track with people who are focussed on a 5km PB when you need marathon specific sessions.

There are so many running clubs around, so have a look on the internet and see what is local to you. They differ from Athletics clubs, Running Clubs, Striders, Joggers and so on, so find one that appeals to you. If you aren't sure which one to pick then head down to your local Parkrun, you're likely to find them all there.

4. Get a Health Check

If you have never run before, or if your exercise regime has been limited before deciding to start training for your marathon, then always see your doctor and explain to them that you are planning on radically changing your exercise habits.

Don't be afraid of time-wasting. It is really important to ensure a healthy heart prior to commencing an endurance event. Getting a full check-up won't take long and will give both you and your family peace of mind.

5. Follow a Plan

A marathon is quite a long way to run. Unless you are a coach it is likely that you aren't really sure where to start your training, that's ok! There are a number of free marathon training plans and pay-to-download plans available on the internet, ranging from 'couch to marathon' all the way to sub-3hour plans.

Choose your plan, check that the description meets your needs.
- Can you already run the minimum specified distance, for example, some plans are designed for people that can

already run for 10 miles without stopping, whereas others will start from zero running experience.
- Are you able to commit the required time and number of sessions each week to be able complete the plan (check how many sessions are planned and how long they take)?
- Do you want to train by time or distance? Some plans will tell you to run for 15 miles whereas others will tell you to run for 2 hours.
- Is the plan targeting your goal?

When deciding whether the plan targets your goal, you should also reconsider whether your goal is realistic. If you have never run before then choosing a plan targeting a sub-3hour marathon is not going to be realistic. If you aren't sure which plan to go for, then try some 'pace 'predictor' calculators on the internet to give yourself a rough idea on what to aim for.

6. Get a Coach

If you don't think that an internet plan is for you and your would like a bit more interaction or would benefit from a more hands-on approach, then think about engaging a coach.

Coaches are not just for the elite runners. Even couch-to-5km runners can benefit from a coach.

If you can afford a coach, then get one. A coach will generally;

- Set your training sessions every week
- Tailor your training to suit the particular marathon you have entered (e.g. if it is a hilly course then they will plan in hill strength sessions)
- Monitor whether you complete the sessions, whether you have done the intervals properly or whether you have just jogged
- Amend your training plan based on your performance
- Motivate you when you are struggling
- Notice when you are getting too stressed or fatigued and amend your plan accordingly to keep you healthy and strong
- Give you advice
- Help you balance life, work, and training
- Give you running-specific stretches
- Explain and recommend running drills
- Give you recovery tips
- Give you race day advice
- Give you guidance on race day nutrition
- Provide tips on your marathon course, tell you which bits to look out for

There is a wide range of offerings from coaches, so spend some time researching coaches and find one that suits you. Things to consider;

- Do you like them? If you get on with someone then you're more likely to adhere to your plan and stick with it.
- How will they send you your training?
- How often will they review and update your training?
- Are they happy for you to contact them with questions about your training, nutrition, injuries, general training-related problems? Some coaches will have plans where you email them just once a week, so check your contact limits.
- What medium are they available on? Phone, Video Call, WhatsApp, Text, Email? Does this suit you?
- What is their method of training?
- Can people recommend them?
- Do they have a website and social media profile where you can see how they work?

Coaches also vary considerably in price, so consider this after you have researched the above variables.

7. **Be Consistent**

One of the major secrets to running a successful marathon is consistency. You could be blessed with all of the natural talents, but if you don't train regularly and consistently then you will be more likely to fail.

This is why low-intensity running is so important. It enables you to run more often, do more miles but put less stress on your body, making recovery faster. Doing regular low impact running will make you faster and it will enable you to run further.

Often runners will miss a few sessions, then go out and run as hard as they can thinking a hard run will make up for it. The truth is that it won't. It's likely to do you more damage, you will need more recovery and you will be at a greater risk of injury.

Aim to stick to your marathon training plan, don't binge-train. Binge-training is hitting it hard for a week then missing a week, then hitting it hard again because you're trying to catch up.

If you search through social media, you will find that the most successful runners are those that run regularly, in all weather, without fail. By successful, I mean those that complete their marathons and then go on to have PB's.

8. Adapt Your Plan

Be prepared to adapt your plan to fit around your life. But understand which sessions can go in succession and which you should avoid doing back to back.

Don't be upset when life 'happens,' and training goes out of the window. It's part of building resilience and adapting.

For a successful marathon, you need to follow and stick to a plan, train consistently and with purpose. Life 'happens' and you will find that things come up that means you can't complete your sessions as planned, a family get-together, a children's assembly, your car might breakdown. That's ok! Learn to adapt, learn to juggle life with training.

If you focus purely on training and neglect everything else in your life, then it can become difficult and you might lose the support from your family and friends. Keep them on-side, they're so valuable for when your training hours increase and you need some support and motivation to get you to the end of that long training run or a long week of building up mileage and effort.

9. Train in Bad Weather

How many times have you planned a training run, opened the front door and to be greeted with dark grey skies, only to turn around and not go out? Stop doing this!

The weather could be bad on race day, you will still have to race (unless it's horrendous!) and if you have avoided training in the wind and the rain all year, then you will not be prepared on race day.

Force yourself to go running when it's wet and windy, make sure you have the right clothing. Wind and waterproof jackets, gloves, long sleeve warm tops and tights, a buff. If you've trained in it then you can most certainly race in it.

Running when it's windy can also be really good training, the added resistance will make you stronger and running downwind can be good for morale.

As an added bonus, you will have the best post-run-high when you've finished!

Caveat: Do not, however, run in extreme weather, please be sensible!

10. Join Strava

Strava is a fantastic community app for runners when used in the right way. Post your runs to it, add a comment and some photos, review your pace and see pace improvements. You can also keep tabs on your mileage.

Add your friends and running buddies and you can celebrate everyone's training successes. You can set your runs to 'private' so only your friends can see, and also set a total privacy zone so that your home address isn't obvious!

Caution, however, to not comparing yourself to others. Don't get sucked into thinking 'Dave's done 8 runs this week, I should be running more' – avoid this mindset at all costs! Stick to your plan and do your own thing. But celebrate and embrace your fellow runners celebrating you too.

The same goes for looking at other people's paces. They may have been running downwind for 5 miles! Don't forget it's an average for the whole session so if you have been doing intervals expect your overall pace to show as slow.

Strava is also excellent for motivating you to run when you're tired or if the weather is bad. You'll see others running when it's raining and tell yourself to get on with your own session and stop being such a wimp!

11. Join Social Media

Let the running community embrace you!

Similar to why you should join Strava, but more involved! The running community on both Twitter and Instagram is amazing. Share your training, diarise your running with photos and comments and get support.

Stuck on something? Ask the community and you'll get a wide spectrum of answers and people willing to help you out.

You'll also find it incredibly motivating. Caution though – it's easy to get addicted and some people offering advice on social media may be less experienced than they appear to be.

To start, try searching keywords; #running #marathon #marathontraining #longrun #intervalrun @ukrunchat is also fantastic for putting questions to a wider audience and join our community @podiumaddict.

12. Train Without Music

Most running races now disallow the use of headphones in races. Some have even banned the bone-conducting headphones too.

If you only train with music, then come race day you will struggle with the silence. Don't condition yourself to rely on your music to get yourself running. Learn to be without it.

Listening to your breathing and footfall are great ways to assess your running form and will give you an early warning of when you are getting fatigued and could do with a bit of fuel.

13. Warm-up

Warming up is essential for every run that you do. Even your long runs. You might think that you will be running so slowly there's no possible need for you to warm your body up beforehand.

A warm-up is designed to prepare your body for exercise. It gets your muscles and cardiovascular system working and changes your mindset.

Without a good warm-up, your body is going from cold and stiff to straight into running. It's a shock to your body, your heart rate will spike unnecessarily, which wastes and burns extra matches. Your muscles will not be ready to extend and work yet, so they are more likely to pull and twinge, resulting in injury.

A basic warm-up should include a pulse-raiser; bring the body from a rested state to a readiness to exercise and some dynamic stretching; stretching through movement. Static stretching should be avoided during warm-ups as your muscles are not ready to be extended yet.

If your training sessions do not have an in-built warm up, then add it in beforehand.

14. Always Cooldown

A cool down is often neglected by marathon-runners. It is essential for the body to recognize that it has finished exercising and to aid recovery. Without a cool down, blood can pool in the legs which can make you feel light-headed and dizzy, your muscles can seize and cramp, making them sore.

A cool-down will help flush through all of the toxins and acids that have built up in the muscles during your run, helping the body to repair and making the muscles less sore in the coming days.

Cooldowns should include decreasing your pulse rate and breathing rate to a more resting state and stretching.

If your training sessions do not have an in-built cool down, then add it on afterward. If you find that you finish your run at home and forget to stretch, then stop half a mile from home and do your stretching there, before taking a really slow walk/jog back home afterward.

15. Train at Your Race Start Time

Get your body used to running at the same time of day as your marathon.

Your body gets comfortable with your daily routine, I don't just mean sleep, but also your digestive system and bowel movements! Train your body to expect to be running at a certain time and try to stick to this as often as you can, particularly for your long training runs.

Training at the same time as your race will also help you to experiment and understand what breakfasts work for you. What time do you need to eat before a run, how much breakfast do you want and how does that feel in your stomach?

It's much easier to get up on race morning and run at 8am if you are used to getting up and running in the mornings. If you only train in the evenings, then it will be a shock to the system on race day!

16. Train on Your Race Terrain

Train on similar terrain to your race.

If you want to go to France, then learn French. If you want to go to Spain, then learn Spanish. Don't go to Spain if you want to learn French. Get it?

It's the same with training for a specific race. If you want to run a really flat fast marathon, then train predominantly on flat roads. Get used to running perfectly paced, fast mile splits for long distances.

If, however, you want to run a hilly off-road marathon, then you will need to find hilly off-road routes for training. Why? Because if you run flat, tarmac routes throughout your training, then all of the little stabilizing muscles and connective tissues that you haven't prepared and trained will go into over-drive, you'll get sore ankles, sore knees, and sore hips because your body is used to running on smooth, flat surfaces.

Equally, running up- and downhill stresses the body in different ways to running solely on a flat route, so make sure you are conditioned for it. You will also need the mental belief and stamina when you are running uphill in the last 6 miles of your marathon, knowing that you have practiced hills and that you are great at them will be a huge confidence boost.

Learning how to run downhill efficiently is especially useful, most people that haven't trained on a hilly course will 'put the brakes on' when they run downhill, slowing them down and causing greater impact through their legs, making them more prone to injury. More people cramp running downhill during a marathon than anywhere else on the course if they haven't practiced it.

17. Run Off-Road

Running on a hard surface can be tough on your joints. Give them a little break by going off-road, whether that's doing laps of a park or finding a trail through the forest.

Running off-road has the added bonus of strengthening your joints, the ground is uneven and makes your stabilizing muscles and connective tissues work a little bit harder than they would on the smooth tarmac. Becoming stronger means less chance of injury.

You will find that 5 miles off-road is much harder and slower than running the same distance on the road. Embrace it and know that the benefit is greater. Gates, stiles and mud will all slow your pace

Running off-road can also be more stimulating and interesting. If you're getting route-fatigue from running the same boring route from your house everyday then get out into the forest, the park or next to a canal and run with nature, enjoy the fresher air and lack of traffic.

18. Cross-train

Running is an impact sport, which means that you put a heavy force through your joints on every stride, there are 40,000 to 50,000 steps in a marathon alone.

Cross-training is the perfect way to train your cardiovascular system without putting added strain on your body. You'll strengthen different muscles, which will help to reduce the risk of injury.

Your cross-training sessions can be low intensity and non-structured, they will still be beneficial.

Try swimming or cycling, enjoy doing something different.

19. Routine

Training can be hard to stick to. If you find a routine, then it helps to keep the momentum going. It also helps family and friends plan a social life to include you because they are aware of when you need to be training.

Life 'happens' so don't stress out if your routine needs changing sometimes, embrace the change, enjoy doing something out of the ordinary.

20. Learn to Pace Accurately

Aim to hit every mile of your long run at the same pace.

But this contradicts advice on Negative Splits (see tip #83)! While it does contradict it, it does emphasize that if you aren't disciplined enough to negative split, then at the absolute minimum, you have to aim for a consistent pace throughout your whole marathon.

The most important message to take home is that you should not get a 5km, 10km, 21km PB in the first half of your marathon. You are almost guaranteeing that you will 'hit the wall' and have a miserable time in the last few miles.

It is so important that you don't get too excited and run fast in the first 13 miles, everyone around you will be buzzing, adrenaline pumping and they'll sprint out of the starting blocks like Usain Bolt in the 100m final. Ignore them, put a lid on your pride and let them go. You will notice that the closer you get to the finish, the more of them you will overtake.

If there is a pacer then aim to stick with them if you can, but keep an eye on your mile splits. Sometimes the pacers can get distracted and you'll find your pace slows for a few miles until they notice and then they will speed up to catch back up to schedule - if you are responsible for your own pacing and not relying solely on someone else, then you will have a successful race. A Garmin virtual partner or race planner can help.

21. Understand the Importance of SLOW

One of the major head-spins of marathon training is running slowly. You have to run slowly to be able to run fast. You have to run slowly in order to make it through the volume of training ahead of you.

Not doing your long slow run is, quite frankly, sabotaging your own race day.

The best ratio between low-intensity training and high-intensity training is 80% low and 20% high. This has been researched extensively and proven to be a winning recipe for endurance athletes. So, go slow for 80% of your training volume and put more effort in for 20%! Wahoo, that's a free pass to go slow (but not on every run).

You should be able to have a full conversation whilst running, not feel short of breath and not need to pause between words. If you can talk but not sing, then you are probably going too fast.

Aerobic capacity is improved during low-intensity training, the body gets better at extracting oxygen from the air that we breathe, it becomes more efficient at transferring that oxygen to the working muscles and therefore releasing energy. This means that the muscle contractions are powered more efficiently too.

Your heart pumps more blood per beat because it gets stronger, your blood volume increases, you get a greater capillary density in your muscles which means that oxygen is circulated to them better.

The muscles will become more efficient at burning fat as fuel, which means your body drills into your fat stores during races – you'll take longer to get tired.

By training at a slower pace for longer, you also increase your mental endurance and stamina. Bonus! You get used to doing the long slow sessions, which is vital for marathon running. -It's basically brain training.

Furthermore, the longer slower sessions and the repetition of movement trains your brain to find more efficient ways of moving. The more you move (e.g. a run stride), the more opportunities you give your brain to find an easier way of making that muscle move. It's not rocket science to recognize that you won't be able to train your brain for long enough if you're hammering hard through a session and have to stop before you meet the time/distance required to start benefiting from the brain training. You need to exercise for long enough to improve your fatigue resistance.

Running at a lower intensity for 80% of the time also means that you are putting less strain on your body. You can increase your running volume (sensibly) without such a high risk of injury. The strain on your muscles and joints is less than it would be when you go fast, which means that you can train for longer, get the miles in. But the important aspect is that at a controlled low intensity, these are NOT junk miles.

One of the biggest benefits, in my opinion, is that you can recover faster from a long, low-intensity session than you do for a medium-length session at moderate intensity or a short session at high intensity. You can run again tomorrow and continue to build your fitness without necessarily needing to take a rest day.

Too much high intensity running stresses the parasympathetic nervous system which means you lose performance and you induce chronic fatigue. Over-training is a bad state to be in and should be avoided at all costs, it can easily ruin your season.

It is hard to slow down. Why? Pride. You think that people are going to judge you when they see you running down the street at a 'snail's pace', you think they're going to mutter 'he's rubbish.' The truth is, they might! But what do you care?! You are running slowly at this particular moment because you CAN run fast, and you are going to run FASTER! You have nothing to prove to these on-lookers, this is your training, not your race. Once you've managed to sweep your pride aside, you can embrace running at a lower intensity. Enjoy it. Take your time to appreciate your run route and take your time to consider your technique.

You get so much more benefit out of your long runs than any other type of training run. You get both the mental and physical benefits. In the most basic of terms, your heart and lungs get stronger, your biomechanics become more efficient, your muscles get stronger and your mental toughness improves. Not only that but you get the perfect opportunity to test your pre-race routine, your kit and your nutrition and hydration. Do NOT miss these sessions!

You must build your long runs up week by week. This doesn't mean that every week you have to go further, you can de-load some weeks and allow your body to recover, rebuild and get even stronger ready for the next long run, but the general trend through marathon training is to build on distance. You do not have to run a marathon before you run the marathon race. You should aim to run continuously for the 'time' you want for your marathon though. If you want to run a 4hr marathon you should have run for 4 hours in training, even if it is at half your intended pace, the closer you can get to the 26.2 miles, the easier it will feel on race day.

As mentioned in the other tips, long runs should be executed at a slow and consistent pace. Aim for a maximum of 5 seconds variation per KM (if you're running a flat course).

Try not to do a lapped course, the temptation can be to not complete the last laps, especially when the weather isn't nice or if they go by your front door!

If you really, really, can't find a ~3-hour block to do your long run, then try doing a double run day. Do half of the run in the morning and the other half in the evening. It's not the best solution, but it can be better than nothing. Do not try and do your long run at a faster pace to get it done quicker.

22. Slow = Slow

If there is one thing you should take home after reading this book, it is that your slow runs should be done slowly!

Building muscular endurance and cardiovascular endurance is key to a successful marathon. By increasing your running mileage you add a lot of extra stress and strain to your cardiovascular system and your muscles, if you stick to a low pace and low heart rate for your long runs, then you will be able to recover faster, be at less risk of injury, less risk of overtraining all while running further.

If you run fast all of the time you are putting tremendous stress on your body, and it will get really, really tired, injuries will increase, your immune system will stop working as efficiently and you will catch colds and bugs more easily. You will find that you start to miss more sessions because of injuries, sickness, and fatigue and your marathon training will be at risk of total failure.

Running slowly can be a bit boring sometimes, try to find an interesting route or find someone to run with.

If you enjoy running with someone then don't allow yourself to run faster because their 'slow' is slightly faster than yours. If you go too fast on your slow runs, then you risk sabotaging your whole training plan.

23. Podcasts Help

If you get really bored on your long slow runs then try listening to a podcast or an audiobook. Avoid music though, listening to someone talking will help you to keep to a slower pace.

Don't listen to something on every long run though, you need to train yourself to run without the noise and distraction. You won't have headphones on race day, so practice this regularly.

24. Celebrate Successes

You should be proud of yourself every time you reach a new distance in training. Celebrate these milestones, they're important successes in your marathon training journey.

You might have found that run really hard, but that makes it even more of an achievement for finishing it.

Share your progress with friends and family, on running forums and social media and enjoy feeling good about your training. It's so important to stay motivated and recognize your hard work and dedication along the way.

25. Add Speedwork

Most of your long runs should be at a nice 'Zone 2' or 'Easy' pace, however adding speed work into your long runs will reap benefits.

It will not only break up the monotony of the long run, but it will make you faster.

It will also help you to adapt to changing pace during your long-distance efforts, much like you might have to in a marathon race; a common example is needing to overtake a slow group that is blocking your way, or being frustrated by the runner on your shoulder that noisily breathes like Darth Vader and you need to escape for the sake of your own sanity!

It's important however to not go crazy with speed work. Speed sessions are the most common for injuries to occur, so make sure you are properly warmed up first and that you aren't trying to match Usain Bolt's speed on your first attempt.

26. Practice Race Nutrition

So many runners will keep their race nutrition until race day. It is incredibly important to train with your planned nutrition. Everybody is different and will react to nutrition products differently. What works for Dave, won't necessarily work for you.

Some people can take on a lot more carbs per hour than others, experiment, find your limits and adjust your plan to suit your body.

Experiment with different brands, products, and timings. Learn how often you should be fuelling and do it during your long runs. Understand how your body reacts to consuming lots of gels on the move – will your stomach feel ok at 22 miles or will you be cramping and bloated? Find out in training and make changes if you need to.

Gels and bars can be expensive but invest in them. Invest in buying more than you need for your race and use them on your long runs. It's just as important to train your body to consume nutrition on the run as it is to run!

Equally, by having your nutrition on your long runs, it will force you to consider how you will carry it. Do you need a race belt? Where will you put the wrappers (you can't just throw them to the ground as that will usually result in a disqualification!). Do you find that you get really sticky from the packets? If so, find a solution. For example, try a squeezy-bottle in your race belt full of gel and sip it as you run.

If you're planning on using salt tablets on race day, then practice this too. Try and do it in the same conditions that you expect to be running in on race day. For example, don't try and take on lots of salt while training in the UK winter because your marathon is in a hot country. You need to simulate the heat and humidity for your body to need and react to the salt as it would for race day. – If you're sweating less then you'll probably need less salt!

27. Do Strength Training

Strength training is all-too-often overlooked by runners. Training loads for marathons are heavy and you might feel as though you have no time to spare to be doing a gym-workout as well.

Strength training doesn't have to mean lifting heavy weight in the gym. Strength training for marathon runners should be aimed at stabilizing your joints, increasing muscular endurance, and increasing muscular and movement efficiency. This can all be successfully achieved through bodyweight exercises at home, no fancy equipment, and no gym memberships.

You could even workout while your dinner is cooking, or in front of the TV.

Strength training will help to decrease your injury risk and will help to make you faster and more efficient.

28. Stretch

The majority of the population spend their time sitting. Your hip flexors get tight, your ankles get tight and your knees don't move all day. Imagine how you feel when you've been sitting for a long time, you are stiff and uncomfortable.

Running needs a mobile body. You don't have to be an Olympic Gymnast, but you do need to have a good range of movement and to be able to move freely.

The key outcome of stretching is the reduced risk of injury, and let's face it, you want to do everything you can to avoid picking up an injury during marathon training.

You will find lots of conflicting articles on the internet about when you should stretch. Before a run, after a run? Both have benefits.

There are two types of stretching, Static Stretching, and Dynamic Stretching.

Static Stretching is when you are still and hold a stretch for a period of time, usually 30 seconds or more, for example, and standing hamstring stretch. Dynamic Stretching is when you stretch through a movement, for example, a leg swing.

It is recommended that prior to running, you warm up with some dynamic stretches, like butt kicks, leg swings and high knees.

Static stretching is best left until after your run when your muscles are warm and able to stretch. Identify any areas that feel particularly tight and focus on these. It's important to stretch these areas properly and not let it build up – that's when an injury can occur.

If you struggle to fit your stretching routine in, then try doing it 2 minutes from home on your way back from your run, then finish with a gentle jog to the house.

29. Foam Roll

You can pick up a foam roller relatively cheaply now, so there's little excuse for not owning one. Foam rolling will help break down knots in your muscles that can limit your movement, think of it as your own personal sports masseuse! It's a great precursor to stretching, by prepping the muscles and stimulating blood circulation.

Foam rolling should be slow and steady, roll slowly until you find a tender point in the muscle, then gently rock back and forth on that point until it starts to release.

You can also use it before and after your runs, or to help stretch and maintain healthy muscles while you are watching TV!

30. Respect the Taper

A taper is cutting your weekly training load prior to your key race. It's one of the most difficult phases of training to implement, everyone reacts to tapering differently, so it might take you a few races to really start to understand what works for you and what doesn't.

Have you heard of the 'Taper Crazies.' When athletes have trained for hours and hours each week for months on end, then they Taper and have so much energy they can't sit still and they're about to burst! You train less, sleep more and eat…sounds pretty awesome, doesn't it? In theory, yes, but you'll feel much like a caged animal. You will worry that every little niggle you feel is a full-blown injury. Your knee will start to burn in pain for no reason, you might start feeling a phantom pain in your calf, athletes are renowned for feeling random aches and pains during taper week. Try not to worry, do not try to do any new and funky stretches to try to eradicate this phantom pain – it will be that weird stretch that does cause you a serious injury!

Tapering is key to a successful race. Your training has built and built over time, preparing you for this race. You have put tremendous, repetitive strain on your body, on your muscles, on your mind, strengthening everything to be able to run and prepare for your marathon. If you don't rest and recover before your big race, then you will be so tired that you will simply not perform at your best.

Think of tapering as a consolidation and recuperation period for your body. It's a time where your body can recover and be at its maximum strength.

You will want to go running, you hate resting, you will feel tetchy and irritable and you'll be chomping at the bit to get some hard, long training sessions in. Don't be tempted. Just because you feel awesome and you have an insurmountable amount of energy doesn't mean that you should use it. Store it. Keep it bottled and unleash it on race day.

If you have been doing a strength routine during training, then start to decrease the weights and the repetitions during tapering or cut out your leg workouts altogether. Stretch and foam roll, do some light training that mirrors your training routine to keep your muscles and mind ticking over but reduce the load and the time. Look after yourself.

31. Do Yoga

Do a runner specific yoga course, it will really help your running. Yoga doesn't have to be a spiritual experience, choose your Yoga teacher to suit your personality and goals and you'll most likely love it.

Yoga requires a lot more strength than you might think. If you engage your muscles properly in the movements and poses, then you will be strengthening your muscles and connective tissues around your joints. We know what this means....less chance of injury!

Many Yoga poses require balance, something that is also essential for running. If you improve your balance and become more aware of your body in space, then your running posture will improve and you will go faster, you'll be much more efficient.

An added benefit of Yoga that is often overlooked by runners is that it teaches you how to breathe. I know, you can already breathe, but are you using your lung capacity fully? Are you breathing in and expanding your belly, filling your lungs with air, or are you actually breathing in and seeing only your chest move? Learning to breathe properly increases the oxygen per breath and therefore the supply to your muscles.

32. Do a Half-Marathon Race

Getting in some race experience is invaluable when it comes to running your first full marathon.

A half-marathon is the perfect race distance, make sure you do this with plenty of time before your actual marathon race, 6 weeks out would be ideal. You'll have enough time to be comfortable at a half-marathon distance and really be able to push yourself to see how your training is coming along. If you've been training consistently up to now, then you're more than likely to hit a PB and get a huge morale boost! Furthermore, you will be able to test out your race kit, routine, and nutrition.

Keep a little diary or journal of what you eat in the run-up to your race, what time you went to bed, how you slept, what time you woke, what time you ate your breakfast and what you had. Note down how you are feeling; excited, nervous, confident? Write down why you feel this. Then, after the race, write a little race report and log your good and bad parts of the race. How many gels you consumed, did you stop for water?

After a few days or a week, look back at your notes and see where your training needs to be altered. Did you struggle on the hills? - Add more hilly routes and hill reps into your training. Was your pacing inconsistent? Spend more time perfecting the art of sticking to a set pace. Did your stomach feel uncomfortable? – What did you eat for breakfast, what gels did you use, did you have too many/not enough? And so on.

If you didn't perform as well as you hoped but felt like you did everything right on race day, then look back through your training logs. Have you completed every session as planned? Are you cutting the last ten minutes of the warm-up off? Address these issues and aim to improve on them.

33. Include Running Drills

Running drills help to condition the mind and muscles into using efficient, mechanically sound running movements that will help to keep you strong, reduce injury, make you run more efficiently and help you to run faster. There really is no reason to miss out on doing running drills.

Drills can be tailored to your running needs, this is where having a coach can be a huge benefit. Your coach can identify the key parts of your running style that would benefit most from certain drills.

34. Don't Change Your Running Style.

Many runners will read blogs about running, watch YouTube videos by elite runners and decide halfway through their training that their running style is all wrong and that they need to change how they run completely to mirror what Mo Farah is doing.

Every person runs differently, Mo Farah's style is completely different from Paula Radcliffe's.

If you try to change your running style during training, then you are very likely to become injured. Your body has strengthened and been conditioned to run in your specific way, if you then change your movement pattern then the little stabilizing muscles will be worked differently, they'll have more load and won't necessarily be strong enough to adapt quickly at the volume of training you are asking them to do.

Think very carefully about whether it is the right time to be changing fundamental aspects of your foot-strike. Changes like these, if you really feel as though you must, are best done when you are at the start of a training plan, if at all.

You can alter little things, like the angle of your arms, relaxing your shoulders, the body angle you run at, but try to avoid big, fundamental changes.

35. Ask for Help

If you have not run a marathon before then you might have hundreds of questions or worries. Don't dwell on them, ask your friends their opinions, but don't always believe everything they tell you! Particularly when it comes to the pace of your training runs; running fast all of the time isn't the answer.

Consider who you are asking and how qualified they are. Many people like to talk as though they are an expert, but be cautious of this. If in doubt, find a coach and ask them.

A great forum to ask for support is @UKRunChat which can be found on Twitter.

It is also important to ask friends and family for help, not just for running advice, but also how to juggle family life and marathon training. You might need some extra rest, so do not be afraid to ask someone to look after the children for a few hours so you can get a much-needed sleep in.

36. Balance Training with Life.

Try not to let marathon training become all-consuming. When you are so focussed on the end-goal it can be easy to neglect your friends, family and prior life-commitments.

Remember that you have friends and family, they want to see you succeed, so don't shut them out.

Marathon training will undoubtedly take up a huge amount of your time and energy, but it is crucial that you allow some time for the other people and events that are important in your life.

It is ok to miss the odd session, do not add extra stress to your life by trying to squeeze everything in. A successful marathon is built on a balance of consistent training, adequate rest, support from friends and family and maintaining a social life that enables you to 'switch-off' and de-stress.

If you are struggling to find a balance, then seek a coach to help you to find a more appropriate running training plan to follow that works with your life and circumstances. There are so many different ways to train for a marathon so don't feel trapped with your one plan, find one that suits you and make it personal.

37. Go to Parkrun

If you keep your running sociable and fun then you will be more likely to succeed.

Parkrun is a fantastic community event and one that runners of all abilities look forward to week on week.

It is a great opportunity to add in some social interaction and a chance to encourage friends and family to try going for a run for the first time.

If you need to run further than the 5km, then try a 'Parkrun sandwich' where you run there, take part in the 5km Parkrun and run home again, or plan it into your long run.

38. Prepare Mentally

This is often overlooked and one of the best tools for success.

If you have never used visualisation before, then give it a go. It can be used in all aspects of life, whether it's before your business presentation to hundreds of people or of you ticking off your last training run.

Get into the habit of visualizing race day before you sleep at night.

- Imagine your pre-race routine that morning.
- See yourself standing on the start line, chatting with family and friends.
- Take note of how excited you are and how that might feel.
- Watch yourself running through the start line.

- See the other runners sprinting off around you in the first 4 miles so that you are prepared for this, watch yourself as you keep to the perfect pace mile on mile and catch them back up again when they get tired.
- Imagine seeing your watch at every mile - it's showing perfect mile splits!
- Imagine yourself getting to the half-way mark and note that you are still feeling strong.
- Then to 20 miles. You have a big smile on your face.
- Picture yourself crossing the finish line and how that's going to feel.
- What emotions will you be experiencing?
- How will you celebrate?

By practicing visualization you are preparing your mind for race day. You are training it to be ready for the marathon and you will feel less apprehensive when you stand on the start line.

It will also help you to sleep the night before the race because you have a routine of thoughts before you go to sleep and you are relaxed about what race-day has in store for you.

Start visualisation early on in your marathon training journey, the more often you do it, then better the outcome will be.

Do this regularly, the best time is either first thing in the morning or before you go to bed. Train your mind for success.

39. Believe

Belief is a key part of getting to the finish of your marathon.

Your training should be planned in such a way that you increase your distance gradually until you reach your marathon race day. Each successful training run should be celebrated, value your achievements and welcome the extra confidence that training run has instilled upon you.

Regularly take a step back and look at your training, admire how far you have come, from running short distances to being disciplined and able to run further week on week. Take confidence in your progress. If you ever have a week where you are struggling, then take time out to look back through your training records and smile at how much you have achieved already. It's a good incentive to carry on.

Don't let anyone tell you that you can't do it. If they try to, then politely decline to listen!

If you have an unsuccessful training run then try not to dwell over it. Everyone will have off-days, it's part of being human. You might be over-tired, becoming ill or just not concentrating due to work or family distractions. Try not to let this bother you and don't go out to attempt to do the same training run again. Let it rest and move on.

40. Remind yourself of 'Why'

When you are feeling tired, sore or a little bit demotivated then remind yourself of the reasons for entering this marathon.

- What motivated you to enter the marathon?
- Are you running the marathon for someone?
- What is your target time?
- Is this marathon as part of training for something bigger?
- How will you feel when you cross the finish line?

You could write these down and pin them to your fridge or save it as your desktop background.

Keep reminding yourself of 'why' and allow it help to keep you motivated.

Share your reasons with your family so they can help remind you too.

41. Write Down your Marathon Concerns

Write down everything you are worried about in relation to your marathon. Then write next to them the answers, solve the problems.

For example, if you are worried about the distance:

<u>Concern</u>

It's a long way!

Answer

I have done all of the training and I am prepared and ready.

If you don't know the answer, then ask a coach or an experienced marathon runner for advice.

Once you have your answers, rip up the paper and throw it away. You have solved the worries and know how to overcome them, try not to dwell on the issues and focus on the positive aspects of your training.

42. Let Missed Sessions Go

Avoid playing catch-up, if you miss a few days of training, do not try to add them in on top of your existing sessions. By doing so, you are likely to experience overload, not allow your body adequate recovery time. You therefore increase your chances of getting injured.

You can often juggle your schedule, but make sure you don't overload yourself.

Keep hard sessions with at least a day in-between, try not to do successive long runs and don't do interval session after interval session followed by a tempo run.

Prioritize the slow-paced, low heart rate sessions and these build your strength and endurance for the marathon distance. These low-intensity runs should be the majority of your training volume.

Your priorities should be; to be able to run 26.2 miles, not get injured, not get ill.

Speed can come as a last priority when you've built a solid base, don't try to rush it.

43. Avoid Panic Training

If you have missed more training sessions than you have completed, then you should seriously consider whether you are on the right path for finishing your planned marathon race.

A marathon is a long way and if you have not been able to complete the planned training then you might make it round, but you could do an awful lot of damage to your body in the process.

If you have not done any training and then decide a few weeks away from your marathon race date that you should begin training last-minute, then don't suddenly run every day for as far and as fast as you can. It takes time to build up your muscles and time for your body to cope with the added stresses of running. Running is an impact sport and needs to be respected.

If you suddenly go from 'zero to hero' then the most likely outcome is illness and injury, both of which are likely to lead to you not making it to the start line.

If you have left it late but are determined to train with the time you have remaining, then do the long, slow sessions, building up the distance in small chunks. Avoid speed training, and avoid ramping up your weekly miles too quickly.

Do everything you can to recover in between your runs, preparing for a marathon like this is likely to lead to you waking up on race morning feeling exhausted before you even reach the start line and is not recommended.

44. Don't Try Anything Funky in the Final Few Weeks

All too often someone will join in with a five-a-side football match the week before race day and twist their knee or pull their groin, ruining their race and all of those months of training!

Equally, don't go for that fish curry at the restaurant next door to your hotel the night before the race, it's just not worth the risk.

The same applies to experimenting with new nutrition, race belts, trainers, socks, pants….everything.

Stick to your tried and tested kit and food. It might sound boring, but it works.

45. Avoid Negative People

You will probably find that when you tell someone you are running a marathon that there are two types of response. One group of people will high-five you and offer endless support and advice, the other group will ask you why and spurt out an endless list of reasons advising you why running a marathon is a really bad idea.

The people who consider it a bad idea are generally people who have never run or exercised before and haven't experienced the joy of training for a marathon and how amazing crossing that finish line feels.

Surround yourself by positive, supportive people. Don't let other people's doubts and insecurities rub off on to you.

You can do this.

46. Stitch

Stitch is one of running's great mysteries. It's cause has not yet been reliably scientifically proven.

Try and recognize patterns of when you get a stitch.

If you get a stitch regularly, then keep a diary of what you have consumed (food and drink; the type and how much and at what time) and what time you train and how you are feeling (stressed, anxious, relaxed, rushed) and try to determine any patterns.

As an example – I tend to only get a stitch when I run with my husband, his 'slow' is my 'fast' so I am running at max-effort for the first 5 minutes while trying to have a conversation with him and I always get a stitch. I avoid these now and rarely suffer from it.

There are many reported reasons as to why a stitch occurs, everyone will have a different explanation.

You will generally find that there is a pattern specific to you, so try to recognise it.

47. Embrace the Tiredness

You will get tired during training. Very tired.

Learn to give yourself extra time to sleep, eat and recover. A successful training program includes time for repair and rest. It's so important that this is not neglected and should be regarded as important as the running miles themselves.

Learn to manage being 'crabby' and short-tempered and don't take your training induced tiredness out on your family. They are not likely to be sympathetic.

Recognize when you are tired and when your mood is affected, try to go for a nap or change your plans to ensure you can rest and recuperate. Make sure you are eating and drinking enough to allow your body to recover.

48. The Hardest Part Of The Marathon Is The Training

Nail the training and the marathon should be easy!

Your marathon will last, on average, 3-6 hours. That is a tiny fraction of the total time you have invested in to training and preparation for the event.

Be really proud of your training, of the hours you have spent running and how hard you have worked to get here. Understanding the importance and value of your training will help you to keep going should you experience low points in the weeks before your marathon.

Stand on the start line knowing that you have done everything possible. Trust in your training plan and trust that your body knows what to do to get you to the finish.

You just need to do what you have practised in training, put one foot in front of the other, consume some fuel, drink and don't forget to smile!

49. Change The Subject

Running will take over your life.

It's a fact that when you start training for a marathon and following your training plan, everything you do will be running-related.

You will find yourself dreaming about running, every conversation you have will ultimately be about your running or your training. This is great and really motivating for you, however, it is important to remember that your family and friends have other interests too (unless, of course, they are all marathon runners!).

Talk about things that don't involve running.

Be considerate about your conversation topics, not everyone will want to know about your 'Runners Trots' or how your nipple rubbed and bled last Thursday.

You need to keep your friends and family on-side as they will help and support you when you're having a tough day and need some motivation to get your trainers on. They can be the drive you need to tick off the training run you've been avoiding.

Talking about non-running subjects will also help to revitalize you, just like your body, your brain needs a rest from running too!

RECOVERY

50. Learn to Rest

Rest days are just as important, if not more important than your running days (provided you have actually run, that is!).

Rest days help to prevent injury and reduce CNS (central nervous system) fatigue. When you train you create microscopic tears in your muscles. This is a good thing because when your muscles repair, they get stronger. The important word in that last sentence is 'repair' – you have to give your body enough time to repair in order to make the gains. If you don't let your body recover, then you'll keep tearing, tiring and fatiguing your muscles, which has the adverse effect, they won't get stronger, you will get slower and ultimately you will get injured.

Rest doesn't just mean putting your feet up, it also includes sleep. If you find that you are not tired, or you are having difficulty sleeping or regularly irritable then you are probably not sleeping enough and you are in danger of over-training.

You need to be cautious and watch out for these signs. Respond to your body when you see them, or ask your family to watch-out for them and to let you know when they think you might need a rest.

If you haven't got a rest day scheduled and you're feeling really run down, irritable, not hungry, desperate to train but have no energy, or you are feeling sluggish and just 'Meh' then it's probably a good idea to take a rest day.

If, however, your body aches and you're a bit tired, then keep to your plan. Learn the difference between the two. If you can't distinguish them, then the best idea is to get a coach to help monitor your health and training load.

In short, if you rest correctly, then you will get faster and stronger.

51. If You Are Ill, Rest.

If you have got a virus then your body is redirecting its efforts to fight that virus and to get you well again. This is part of why you feel so tired when you start to get ill – your body is focussing its resources elsewhere.

If you have just got the sniffles then you are probably ok to still go running, the adrenaline released (the epinephrine) is said to be a natural decongestant, but keep it sensible and don't go for your long run or hard intervals.

If, however, you are feeling the illness in your chest, feeling weak, short of breath or have other symptoms then it is always best to take a rest day and let your body recover. Seek advice from your doctor.

Training while you have a virus may result in the virus worsening and you becoming even more unwell, so please be careful and always seek advice from a medical practitioner if you are ever in doubt.

One rule banded about by runners is the 'Neck Rule' whereby if you feel it above your neck only, then you are ok to run. If you feel it below your neck, then take a rest day. I am not a doctor, so don't take this as a science, always seek medical advice if you are unwell and still want to train.

52. Respect Injuries

Avoid the urge to 'google-doctor' an injury or assume it's 'XXX' because Dave down the pub has something similar.

If you have a pain that is not expected, then seek professional advice as soon as you can. It is likely that the longer you persist with training on a small niggle, the bigger the problem is going to get.

Having a professional diagnose the source and cause of the pain is essential. You need to understand how to treat the injury, whether you can still train while injured, how long recovery will be and whether you need any additional support, such as a physiotherapist or a sports massage.

Quite often, the underlying cause of the pain is not at the site of the pain itself. This is one of the reasons why you need to get your injuries seen by a professional.

Do not try to 'run through' the pain. This will, more often than not, cause a small injury to become worse, lengthening the healing time.

If you are told to rest, then rest!

53. Get a Sports Massage

Sports massages are great for maintaining healthy muscles and joints throughout your marathon training. It will help your muscles to recover and keep your joints moving through their full range of motion, reducing the risk of injury and could even help you to recover from an injury more quickly.

Sports massage therapists are all very different in their approaches and the amount pressure they apply. You might need to try a few before you feel comfortable with one, seek some recommendations from other runners and ask the therapist what their primary client's sport is, for example; if they mostly help rugby players then their experience and knowledge on marathon runners' legs might not be as good.

Sports massages are not relaxing, so do turn up to your appointment and expect aromatherapy oils, panpipes and some soothing, gentle massage across your back and shoulders. You can expect elbows in your glutes and pressure on your muscles, stretching and manipulating the muscles. Don't be afraid to tell your masseuse if the pressure is too much, it's not a competition to see if you can brave the pain.

Sports massages can be expensive, but many offer a bulk-booking discount, so try to purchase these where you can.

You will often find sports massages being offered before and after your marathon on race day, on-site. As mentioned above, sport massage approaches can vary widely, so have an on-site pre-marathon sports massage at your own risk.

A post-marathon sports massage is, however, a good idea. It will help to flush out the toxins that have built up in your muscles and will help you to recover. Try to get one as soon as possible after you finish, booking is often available.

54. Refuel ASAP

Replenishing the energy you have used is vital for your recovery.

Aim to have either a recovery drink or a small meal as soon as you get back from your training run. This replenishes the carbohydrates, protein and fluids that you will typically have lost during your run. Your body needs to recover and repair, so make sure that it has enough fuel and nutrients to be able to do this.

Undereating can be detrimental to your running progress and to your long-term health. If you are trying to lose weight during your marathon training, then it is of utmost importance that you understand the amount of calories and which nutrients you need each day, do not try to guess this and seek advice.

All athletes should learn how much you need to consume and which types of foods are best. If you are unsure, then consult a sports dietitian to give you a personalized plan.

KIT

55. Have At Least Two Pairs Of Running Trainers

We all have a pair of trainers that are our absolute favourite. We have to move away from that mindset for marathon training. If you love a particular style of a trainer then get another pair. Alternate them through your training and don't save a pair for race day.

Rotate through your trainers, this not only gives them all an even wear, but it also keeps your feet working and strong. Furthermore, if your favourite pair of trainers get lost or ruined, then it won't be the downfall of your race.

It's also great to have a variety of trainers in different styles, this will help your feet to maintain all-over strength and not become weak in an area where a particular shoe offers support.

Different shoes will support your feet in different places, meaning that the small stabilising muscles and tendons will work slightly differently in each pair.

You will also need a pair of trail shoes for when you run off-road, these are often more supportive than a road trainer and have more grip.

56. Get A Running Gait Analysis

When buying your trainers, have a run analysis at the shop. Ask the assistant to evaluate how your foot hits the ground as you run and then ask them which type of trainers will suit your foot strike and running style.

Run analysis are usually free at good running shops and will normally take around an hour. You will likely be asked to do some short runs (a couple of minutes) on a treadmill or outside and then try a selection of trainers, run in them again and perhaps try some more. Take your time, get it right.

Wear suitable clothing when you go trainer shopping, dress with the expectation to run – jeans wouldn't be appropriate! Similarly, wear the same socks that you intend on running in, not your comfy ski-socks!

It's best to find a well-recommended running shop to purchase your marathon trainers from. Try to avoid going to the big sports shop where the staff are likely to have limited running-specific knowledge and do not just pick the trainers that you think look cool. Your body will not thank you for it! Running shops carefully employ their staff because of their passion for running and understanding of how important a properly fitted pair of trainers are to your success.

Take your time and choose carefully.

57. Socks

If only socks were just socks. They aren't. You can get toe socks, double-lined socks, ankle socks, trainer socks, compression socks, knee-length socks, heat holding socks, cooling socks…the list is endless.

Socks are a very personal thing. Everyone's feet are different, your trainers will feel different with different socks on too, so don't just buy what your mate wears.

Make sure to try lots of varieties of socks on your long runs and find the type that feels the most comfortable. Try not to keep a brand new pair of socks for race-day. Race in worn socks (but clean ones!).

It is also vital to wear your race-day socks with the trainers that you run and race in. Comfy socks might rub on the insoles of your favourite pair of trainers differently or cause extra heat or friction, particularly when running downhill.

58. Support – Sports Bras and Boxers

Men – wear some good fitting pants or boxers and make sure they fit snugly (without chafing) and support you sufficiently.

I was once told a story from a male friend who had run an ultra-marathon; his greatest pain throughout the race was his testicles, they were not supported while he was running. He finished the race, but had to physically hold them in his hands to support them.

Women – have a professional bra fitting and buy a sports bra that fits correctly. There are many different varieties of sports bras on the market, a heavy-duty level of support is recommended for running. If you have a larger chest then consider the different shoulder strap options. Some of the cross-backed sports bras can put strain on your trapezius muscles and cause neck and headaches. Also think about whether there are seams on the sides, will these rub your arms as you run?

59. Wear Less

When you are getting ready for your run and see the grey skies outside, your instinct will be to put on another layer.

Don't do this! You will get very warm running and becoming too hot will slow you down.

It's also much harder to run with lots of kit on, it's heavy, bulky and weighs you down. Think about how aerodynamic cyclists try to be, the more clothing that flaps in the wind, the more resistance you are moving forwards against. It is the same with running, wear less baggy items that will flap in the wind and try not to weigh yourself down.

Start practicing with different combinations of base layers and light windproof jackets, all of which should fit you comfortably.

My recommendation is that for most runs, wear shorts, then either a vest, t-shirt or a long-sleeved running top. You'll probably want tights in the winter months though.

Your clothing and temperature will be different for each type of training run; intervals, long slow runs, etc. Practice with layers, experiment and find what works best for your body temperature. You are better to be a little bit chilly when you start than to be overheating half way through your run and struggling to cool down.

60. Be Weatherproof

If you have the right kit, then there will no longer be many excuses to allow you to skive from a run in the rain.

Don't let yourself wimp out of getting wet, it's only rain.

If you avoid training in bad weather then when the weather is dark, wet and windy on race day, you will struggle. Not necessarily physically, but mentally. Your brain will be telling you that it is too wet, or too cold or too windy so you won't perform well, or that you should just not go to the marathon at all. Train in all weather and be confident that you can perform in it.

Be prepared for everything. Learn how to layer up your clothing to keep you warm and dry, you don't have to do hours of research, ask in any good running shop and the assistant will be able to give you a full, quick explanation about which items to choose and offer various different pricing options.

Try not to go for the cheapest rain jacket though, it is likely to leak.

Running in the rain can be really enjoyable, there is something quite liberating about it, so give it a try.

61. Chafing

Chafing is where your skin rubs together, or where something you wear rubs against your skin, making it sore or bleed.

Chafing may seem like a minor and silly issue, but it can easily ruin your race. People have dropped out of marathons because the chafing has become so painful they can no longer move. Don't let this be you.

Chafing hot spots are;

- Nipples (more so with men)
- Under the arms, for women; where your sports bra meets your upper arms when they swing, and for men, where the seam of your t-shirt is.
- Between your thighs.
- Between your calves, if they touch.

- Back of neck, where the label is in your running top
- Between your bum-cheeks
- Men – Perennial area.

The easiest step is to avoid race-day chafing in the first place.

Never wear new kit on race day. This includes pants, socks, shorts, running top, race belt, gloves, headbands. EVERYTHING must have been worn together in a full dress rehearsal on a long run before the race.

On race day, it is also recommended to put a coating of Vaseline around the bits that you suspect might chafe. If you have already tested your kit, then this shouldn't be necessary as you'll be confident that you will be ok. If the pre-race jitters have got hold of you and a little bit of Vaseline will calm your nerves, then go for it.

If you get really sore nipples, then pop plasters over them.

Vaseline is normally available from the medics around the marathon course, so if you get really sore, don't be afraid to ask for some!

62. Be Aero

Being 'Aero' is usually a term associated with Triathlon. However, I believe it is equally as important for runners too.

Imagine walking down the road into gale-force wind with a big coat on, unzip your coat and hold it out to both sides. You will be blown backward because the wind is hitting a greater surface area and will therefore affect you more, imposing a greater force to push you backwards with. This is the same as running and wearing big baggy t-shirts and shorts.

If you wear tight-fitting clothing, you will be more streamlined and will be able to move forward through the air and wind with less effort.

Do you really want to waste energy for the sake of wearing a baggy t-shirt or a pair of shorts over your running tights?

63. Dress Rehearsal

Do some long runs in exactly the same kit, use your race nutrition at the planned miles or time intervals and eat your planned breakfast as you would do on race day. Even try your pre-race day evening meal the night before.

We all love new running kit. You feel amazing every time you wear something new and you want that feeling on race day. Don't do it! Quite often, there will never be a problem with a new piece of kit, but you can guarantee that the one time it is a problem, will be on marathon race day.

At the risk of repeating myself, make sure you train in your race kit, it doesn't have to be every session but aim to do at least two or three of your long runs in all of the gear that you expect to wear on race day. Be aware of any discomforts; is it rubbing a bit under your arm after nine miles? What has caused it? Make a note as soon as you return from your run, you are likely to forget if you wait until after your shower.

Practice with your nutrition, ensure that it doesn't make you feel ill or bloat your stomach. Make sure you know how you will carry your gels on race day; pockets, race belt, tucked in under your bra strap? Where are you going to put your used wrappers?

Aim to have a few rehearsals of race weekend, try to emulate the 2 days before race day, eat the meals you have planned, see whether it sits on your stomach in the morning or makes you feel bloated, are you rushing to the loo?

Figure out whether you are eating enough breakfast before your long runs, or whether you are eating too much and it's making you uncomfortable. Do you need to eat earlier or less sugary foods?

64. Let Them Shout Your Name

Wear a running top with your name on it for race day.

When you are 19 miles into your marathon and might be starting to feel a little bit tired, there is nothing more motivating than the crowd cheering you on by name.

You will be amazed at how many people will read your name from your clothing and direct their love and support at you to help you on your way. Runners and their families are pretty awesome like that!

Don't be shy! Wear your name with pride and absorb the energy they are sending you. You don't have to wave and thank them all, they'll know by your face that you've been grateful for their help, even it looks like a grimace!

Equally, if you are feeling great and you pass a runner with their name visible, then call it out and give them a thumbs-up, praise or a nod of support.

If you have joined a running club, then wear your club vest on race day. Every club member will cheer you on and so will their supporters, it is an amazing feeling.

NUTRITION

65. Count Race Day Calories

Once you have decided which fuelling system you will use for your marathon; which gels, jellies or food you want to carry with you, then work out how many calories a serving will provide. Calculate how often and much you will need to consume to successfully keep you energized until the end of your marathon.

Each manufacturer will have a guide on how regularly you should fuel with their specific products during an endurance event, read their guidelines, trial it in training and adapt it where necessary to suit your needs.

Do not just copy what your friends do!

One of the major mistakes that people make is to wait until they feel tired before taking a gel. By this time, it will be too late, you will already be in deficit and will be playing catch-up with energy. Start your fuelling plan straight from the start of your day and fuel regularly, even if you feel great. This gives you the best opportunity of staying strong until the finish.

If your stomach is feeling uncomfortable, then you can try sipping on gels over time, rather than trying to gulp each sachet down all at once.

If you have practiced fuelling on your long runs, then you should not have any nasty surprises on race day.

66. Eat More

Ensure you eat enough calories in your daily life – it might be a shock that most runners under-eat.

Eating enough is incredibly important. Find out how many calories you should be consuming daily for your size, gender and build, daily activity (i.e. desk working/active labour) then add in the calories that you are burning through exercise.

You may be trying to lose weight while training, that's ok, but don't starve yourself. It is essential that you consume enough calories from all of the food groups to ensure that your body can function, train and recover.

It might seem extravagant but seeking a nutritionist or dietitian to guide you on your basic calorie intake can make the difference between struggling in your marathon and nailing it.

If you struggle to consume enough calories, then consider adding in protein and recovery shakes on top of your meals, do not supplement real food for shakes though, as a general rule of thumb, there is nothing better than real food.

67. Eat breakfast

Race day breakfast is so important. Many people struggle to eat a full and nutritious breakfast in the early hours of race day morning. It is often a consequence of not having practiced it, plus a surge in race morning nerves and adrenaline.

It is vital that you eat enough before your marathon race. If you start your marathon under-fuelled, then you will be on 'catch-up' with your nutrition throughout the whole race and you will likely suffer for it towards the end of your marathon.

Practice eating different breakfasts before your long training runs. Get to know what works for your body, you might find that your favourite breakfast does not sit well in your stomach when you run. Do not be stubborn, sacrifice your favourite breakfast and try to find something new.

Practice the timing of your breakfast, how many hours before your run do you need to eat for your stomach to feel settled?

68. Prepare to Feel Hungry

You are likely to feel incredibly hungry during your marathon training. Snacking and eating regularly will really help you, try to find some recipes to make healthy energy-rich snacks to help you train and recover.

Ensure you know how much you should be eating to cope with your training load and recovery, eat the right foods and add in protein shakes where you need a top-up. As mentioner earlier, don't rely on shakes alone.

Eat real food and enjoy eating, knowing that your body will be thankful that it will be able to repair your muscles.

69. Hydrate Properly

Hydration is one of the biggest problems that runners experience. Why? Because the population, in general, are massively dehydrated in their day to day lives.

Hydration is not just water, it is also the combination of different salts and minerals to help your body to function effectively.

Dehydration will negatively affect your running performance and will also slow your body's ability to recover, meaning that you are more likely to get injured and ill.

It is also suggested that being dehydrated increases the risk of cramping. You do not want to get a cramp during your marathon, so pay particular attention to your salts and hydration levels.

You lose a lot of water through running, not just through the energy process in your cells, but also as your body becomes warm, it will need to lose some of this heat through sweating.

If you think you sweat more than the usual individual, or if you think that your sweat is particularly salty, then I would recommend getting 'sweat-tested' to learn how much extra hydration you will need to be able perform at your optimum level.

Equally, it is important not to over-hydrate. Do not drink for the sake of drinking. Not only will drinking too much before and during your run make your belly feel sloshy and uncomfortable, but it will also put you at risk of hyponatremia which can be the cause bloating and nausea in the mild cases and much worse, ending in hospitalisation, in severe cases.

I would recommend being guided by thirst during your race, if you are thirsty then have a sip of water at the aid station, drinks with added sodium are recommended. Try not to gulp down cups of water. Have a little bit at a time and gauge how you feel each sip.

Something to bear in mind is that Researchers at the Baylor College of Medicine in Houston concluded that the drugs ibuprofen and aspirin impaired the body's ability to excrete water in marathon runners. This means that your body retains water, is unable to cool down and releases heat properly and thus increasing the risk of hyponatremia. Many runners insist on taking ibuprofen with them on the marathon, it's not something that I would suggest and hopefully the above study makes you consider whether that choice is right for you.

Learn how your body sweats, how much hydration you need and understand the different requirements in different climates.

70. Drink on The Move

Most marathons will give out water at aid stations in little plastic or paper cups, they are notoriously difficult to drink out of when on the move.

If you can, practice it, there is a technique that increases your rate of success, getting at least a little bit of water in your mouth, rather than all over your face and in your shoes.

Squeeze the top of the cup so it almost folds in half, then drink from the newly made corner.

Try really hard not to spill water down your legs and into your trainers. Running with wet shoes and socks greatly increases the chance of getting blisters.

If you need to cool down by pouring water over your head then lean slightly forwards or backward before you tip, reducing the amount going into your shoes.

71. Fuel Properly

Think about what you're eating the few days before race day. Will it sit horribly in your stomach when you are trying to run? For example, red meat has a reputation for taking a long time to digest.

If you have a week of takeaway in the lead up to your marathon then you are likely to feel bloated and uncomfortable for your race.

Take note of what foods make you feel sluggish and lethargic, bloated and uncomfortable during training and avoid these, particularly in race week. Equally, if you feel light and energized, then remember what you have eaten and add this into your regular meal plans.

The most important meal is breakfast on race day. Experiment with what makes you feel good, how you feel running after eating it and how much of it you can eat.

Consider making a food diary for a couple of weeks and note what you have eaten, along with how you felt on your training run. You will start to see patterns emerge with your food choices and energy levels.

72. Reduce Alcohol

While you do not need to give up alcohol completely for marathon training, it is absolutely recommended.

An occasional drink will not necessarily do too much damage to your marathon dreams, but it certainly won't do you any favours.

Alcohol is said to deplete the body's ability to consume glucose, which means that it is less efficient at absorbing energy. That is not what you want when you're training consistently for an endurance event where energy is vital to your success.

You will also find that you feel more focused, be able to get out of bed for your morning training runs and recover faster when you are not drinking alcohol.

Furthermore, there are a lot of calories in alcohol, so if you are running to help you lose weight, then alcohol should be one of the first things that you cut out (or significantly reduce) when you set your goals. It's an easy win.

THE RACE

73. Check the Weather

The weather on race day is non-negotiable. It is what it is.

Keep an eye on the weather forecast in the week running up to your marathon and be prepared. Do not obsess over it though, you will have trained in all weather, so it should not greatly affect your race.

Do not leave it until race morning and be surprised that it's raining with strong winds. Know the forecast, have the right kit with you and do not let it affect your confidence.

74. Read the Race Pack

Take some time to read through the Race Pack, don't assume that you know everything because you have done it before, or you know someone from running club that has told you everything already. If there is an Athlete Briefing, go to it.

Race packs are prepared and distributed for a reason. There are so many important nuggets of information in there that will help you to have an easier race day.

- Make sure you know how to get your race number and timing chip; will it be posted to you or do you need to find the registration desk? What are the opening times?

- Understand the route. Where are the hills, is there a hidden dogleg that might demotivate you if you didn't know it was there?

- What nutrition is being provided on course?

- Where are the aid stations?

- Are there first aid points?

- Where is the bag drop?

- Is there a cut off time?

- Where are the toilets?

- Which roads are closed on race day?

- Where should I park in the morning?

- How will the start work? Are there funnels to queue up in at the start based on finish time targets?

- Will there be pacers? If so, for what finish times?

- How does my timing chip attach to my shoe or my shirt?

- Am I allowed to wear headphones?

- Where should my friends and family watch?

- If I need to drop out, what should I do?

- Are there distance markers along the course? Are these in miles or kilometres?

75. Learn the Course

Every marathon is different. You should aim to adapt your training to fit the marathon course that you are aiming to complete.

For example, The Wales Marathon is incredibly hilly, you may need to adapt your target time to take in to account the hill difficulty and that it will increase the time to cover the same distance, especially if you aren't skilled at running downhill. You will also need to run up and down hills during your training, a lot! If you only run a flat course during training then your body may struggle with added strain on your calf muscles and hip flexors on race day. Psychologically, if you know you can make it to the top of a steep hill then you are already there. Furthermore, training on hills will also allow you to understand your effort, you will slow down going uphill to make sure you don't over-exert yourself (or burn too many matches), equally, you may go faster downhill because you relax and let gravity help. Learn how to adjust your speed to keep a consistent effort output.

Learning the course will also help to avoid any unexpected or demotivating surprises. For example, at Brighton Marathon, you feel like you are almost at the finish and you just need to run to the power station to loop around to the finish line. The Power Station is a really long way away. Be prepared for this and do not let it demotivate you.

Knowing the course is also important for nutrition planning, you should know exactly where the water and feed stations are so you know how much fuel to take on board before the next one.

Equally, some marathons will not offer aid stations at all, you will need to carry your own food and drink, so be prepared!

76. Plan your Pre-Race Travel

Getting to the race can induce stress and waste vital energy on race morning. Plan your travel in advance.

Do you need to travel to the race and stay over the night before? It might only be a 90-minute drive, but that could be a really early start and driving isn't the best preparation to run a marathon!

How will you get to the start line on race day, where is parking and how far will you have to walk?

Check which roads are closed for the race and what time they open/close. Do you need some change for parking?

77. Plan your Race Day

Learn where registration, bag drop, port-a-loos, family meetups are in advance.

Decide what you need to do and in which order, by doing this you avoid running back and forth around the start area, wasting energy.

78. Plan How You're Getting Home

This is often overlooked in race planning. You are likely to be quite tired after your marathon, so consider how you are going to get home after your race.

Have a plan B ready if you have planned to walk or jog home, your legs may feel more tired than you had anticipated.

You might want to know the bus routes or have a taxi number handy just in case you are really tired.

Make sure you have some cash in your bag at the finish, you ma need it and having it ready provides some reassurance and saves you from finding a cashpoint when you don't need to walk any further on tired legs.

79. Focus on The Finish

Try not to dwell on your finish time.

Runners are prone to putting pressure on themselves by setting a target time and worrying that they will not achieve it.

Set yourself a realistic goal; a time that your training and ability reflects, not the time that your mate is aiming for.

Do not compare yourself to other people and worry that your time should be the same or faster than theirs. You do not know what their running history is, what their training schedule is like, how much time they have for recovery etc.

When you start your marathon, aim for consistent mile splits, try not to worry about the overall time. If you hit your mile splits then the time will happen by itself.

If you start to struggle to reach your mile splits and fall behind, then that's ok too. Adapt your plan, don't try to catch up and run faster for a few miles, you'll only make yourself slower at the end because your matches have been burned.

Finish times will also be affected by the weather, how busy the course is, whether there has been an incident on the course that has slowed everyone down and a million other variables.

You will often find that if conditions have been difficult then the whole field has run slower that year.

80. Complete the Emergency Information

Always complete the emergency information on the back of your number, you never know when you might need it, even if you have no known medical concerns.

Not completing this could delay your medical treatment or delay your family being contacted should you get injured.

Family really worry when you tell them to expect you at a certain time and you don't arrive, make sure they can be contacted should something unplanned happen.

81. Have a Bin Liner for the Start

Have a bin liner ready to wear at the start to keep you warm.

Granted, bin liners are not environmentally friendly and the running community seems yet to find a disposable alternative to this tip (if you do have any, then please do share!), however, standing at the start line of a marathon, after your warm-up, can be a really cold experience. A simple bin liner, prepared with holes for your head and arms, is a fantastic piece of apparel. It will really keep you warm, protect you from the wind and help conserve your valuable energy while you are waiting to start.

Bin liners are disposable and you can whip it off as you start to move closer to the start line. Most marathon starts tend to have somewhere for your rubbish along the funnel chute, so take advantage of it and throw your liner in the bin.

As an alternative, take a top with you that you would otherwise have thrown away, use it to keep warm, then put it in the bin as pass.

If, however, you have friends or family standing at the side of the start chute, then wear your coat or jumper and pass it to them before you start.

82. Take Loo Roll

Have a stash of toilet paper with you so you can use the portaloo before the race starts.

There are not many more experiences worse than entering a portaloo before a race, after hundreds of other people with nervous tummies. Be prepared. If you can, make sure you have 'expelled' prior to arriving at the race venue, but you will likely need to go again before your race.

Toilet paper is like gold dust in event portaloos, so make sure you have a little stash ready for your visit. If you don't need it after all, then find a worried face in the queue and donate it.

Leave yourself plenty of time before the start to visit the toilet, the queues are often very long and take time to move.

83. Negative Split

This is where most marathon runners fail! You have to start 'too slowly'.

It is race day, you have stood on the start line chatting away to the guy or girl next to you and find out they're aiming for the same time. "Awesome, we can run together!" The starter horn booms and you all move forward. Your new friend is already 10 paces ahead of you and you are scrambling to keep up. Don't!!

It is so easy to get carried away at the start of the race. You are stacked full of energy; your muscles are primed and about to burst with strength after your taper week and your adrenaline is off the charts! REIGN IT IN.

Think about it like this...you have a box of 26.2 matches. Every match is equal. Every match is worth one mile at your goal marathon pace, the pace you have successfully trained at. If you want to go faster than your set pace, you will burn more than one match. If your marathon target pace is 10-minute miles, and you get so excited at the start that you run at 7min30sec miles for the first 4 miles because you 'feel great', then that's 1.25 matches a mile. After 4 miles you are 2 whole matches short of a marathon. You can't get those matches back, you will hit the wall and quite frankly, have a miserable time. Please don't do this!

Generally, if you feel like you are going too slow over the first half-marathon, then you are probably doing it right!

Learn to negative split and practice it. A negative split is a term used when the second half of your race is faster than the first half. Negative splits are encouraged for marathon runners because it makes you conserve your energy during the first portion of your race, reducing the energy consumption and effectively banks it for the last part of the course. Meaning you are less likely to 'hit the wall' and more likely to finish strong.

84. Run Consistently

The key to a successful marathon is a consistent set of mile splits. Have you seen the mile splits of the elite marathon runners? They are normally hitting each mile within seconds of the previous mile, if they speed up, then it's only at the end of the marathon (to get a negative split).

Marathon running is all about managing your energy levels. To do this effectively, you need to control your effort and pace.

"It's a marathon, not a sprint"

We have all heard the above saying, haven't we? It's true, it *is* a marathon, so you need to take it steady. Plan your goal time, a realistic and achievable goal time which is based on your training pace and then calculate what this is per mile.

You want to hit this pace EVERY single mile. No faster and no slower. A great motivational tool is to have a pace chart, know what time you should be getting to each mile at and be motivated by hitting your pace targets. The first 13 miles at your goal pace should seem too easy, understand this and stick to the plan. Practice consistent running during your training runs. If you are not running every mile within 5 seconds or your target pace, then focus on pacing and controlling your speed until you can do it. It is essential.

Yes, I know the above tip tells you to 'Negative Split' but if you are unable to do this, then aim for consistency.

Did you know....you can get temporary tattoo race pace charts now. Stick them to your arm for an easy-to-reference guide on race day.

85. Fuel and Hydrate Immediately

Don't wait until you feel thirsty or hungry or tired before you drink or eat during the race. It is too late by this time.

Keeping on top of your nutrition and hydration is key to a successful marathon. If you ignore your need to fuel and hydrate and remember later on in your race, when you are feeling tired, cramping or struggling to concentrate, then it's too late. No matter how much fuel you take on in one go now, it's too late to rescue your race. At best, you will just make it to the finish.

If, however, you start fuelling and hydrating from the moment you cross the start line, then you are maintaining your energy throughout the race. You are not crashing and then trying to get yourself back up to a level where you can function again. The aim is to keep a reasonably constant supply of energy to your body.

You will be amazed at the difference it makes to your long runs in training too. If you fuel and hydrate properly on your long runs then not only will you have practiced carrying and dispensing your nutrition ready for race day, but you will also gain in confidence. The long runs will no longer seem as hard because you have the required amount of energy.

86. Sing

Pick some songs that motivate you and make you smile. Sing these in your head.

3-6 hours with only your own thoughts can seem like a long time. Make sure you have spent some time on your long runs without your headphones. Learning to be with yourself is a key part of marathon training.

Find something you enjoy to focus your thoughts on. Find some songs that you can repeat to get you through the tough bits, they might be motivational, or they might mean something to you personally. For example, 'I would walk 5 hundred miles, and I would walk 5 hundred more…' or 'I'm having such a good time, I'm having a ball! Don't stop me now!' or perhaps if you feel the cold, you could sing a heat-focused song and imagine being warm; 'It's getting hot in here…' Find what works for you.

Try to avoid hearing annoying songs or mantras just before you start your marathon. The last thing you want is to have that song whirring around your head for 26.2 miles! Have something ready to cancel it out with.

87. Talk to yourself!

Give yourself a 'Yeah' or a 'Whoop' when you hit a mile, remind yourself that you've done the training and 'I can do this' tell yourself to 'slow down' at the start and 'speed up' at the end.

Remind yourself that 'You'll catch him later' as he sprints past you in the first mile!!

88. Walk If You Need To

It's ok to walk during your marathon, don't be embarrassed or feel ashamed. Walking to the finish is much better than not finishing at all!

If you can, swing your arms a bit harder and turn it into a power walk, get to the finish faster.

Aim not to stop and avoid standing still at all costs. Stopping allows your blood to pool in your legs after exercise, which can make you feel feint or dizzy. It also gives your muscles an opportunity to seize up as they cool down.

Always keep moving, no matter how much you would love to pause or rest.

89. Smile!

It is well known that smiling makes everything easier. If you smile while running your marathon then you will not only enjoy it more, but your whole body will feel more relaxed, making your running that little bit more efficient.

Smiling also encourages the marathon crowds to give you an extra cheer, it will encourage other people smile back at you, and will give you a boost.

Never under-estimate the power of a smile, either towards someone else who is struggling to help them on their way or for yourself.

90. Take Less

Avoid carrying too much. It is too easy to think of all of the possible problems you might have on your marathon and pack your race belt full of 'essentials.'

Only carry the basics with you, you should be able to get anything else on the course.

You will not need plasters or Vaseline as most marathon courses in the UK have first aiders spotted around the course with full medical kits.

You will need to carry your nutrition with you, but only if the marathon course doesn't supply the nutrition you want. Read the race pack in advance to see what they offer.

You shouldn't need to carry a drink. Aid stations are usually regularly spaced throughout the course, so check the race pack and learn where they are. Carrying a drink will weigh you down and slow you down. Do you really need it on you at all times?

Don't carry too many clothes either, be prepared to run the whole marathon in just the kit you are wearing. If you think you might take something off halfway around, then it's easier to just not wear it in the first place then have to carry it.

91. Beware, Sunburn

Running a marathon can be a long day. Always put sunscreen on before you start, even if it's cloudy. (Granted if it's torrential rain in the middle of winter, this won't necessarily apply!)

Many people have got sunburnt during a spring marathon, don't let this be you.

Just be careful applying it above your eyes, if you get sweaty it can run it to your eyes and sting.

92. Absorb The Atmosphere

Keep your head up and look around you. You might be amazed at just how electric the atmosphere can be on marathon day. Keep your head up and take everything in.

You will see people dressed as Lobsters, carrying Fridges, running in Swimming Trunks.

There are often bands along the route, playing in all weathers. Enjoy the crowds and the support and absorb their energy.

Read the home-made signs, allow yourself to chuckle at them.

Give the children high-fives, they love it and it will give you an extra boost too!

93. Have a Plan-B

If something isn't going to plan then be prepared to change your goals 'on the fly'.

Marathons rarely go exactly to plan. We have all seen the elite runners, even they have disasters; like Paula Radcliffe stopping for the loo over a drain. Be prepared!

If something unusual happens then try not to let it panic you, think on your feet about how to solve it and revise your mile targets to something more achievable.

It's not always bad things that happen, you might find that you have a huge tailwind along one part of the course which propels you forward much faster than anticipated, with much less effort. You turn the corner and suddenly you can barely step forward into the headwind on the next leg. Revise your mile times and don't exhaust yourself trying to keep to the pre-planned times, don't be disheartened and give yourself a little pat on the back for the miles you have already completed.

You might lose your nutrition, all too often you will see gels that have fallen from runners' belts strewn across the road. If you know what the marathon course is offering, then make sure you stop at the aid station and grab some food, gels or energy drink there. It might make your belly feel different from what you are used to so sip or nibble it slowly as you run, this way it doesn't sit in your stomach in one unexpected lump.

You may also notice that many of the runners around you haven't consumed their nutrition as they planned, and they have some to spare in the last 6 miles. Don't be scared of asking if they have anything you could have, explain quickly to them that you lost yours. The worst they can say is 'no.' Don't give them your life story though, be succinct and friendly.

If you feel unwell on race day, then listen to your body. You will know, deep down, whether you are fit to race. Don't push it when you are feeling ill, a marathon is a long way.

Don't forget, that you will have signed a disclaimer when you entered the marathon to confirm that you will only run if you are fit and well. It is your responsibility. No one will think less of you if you do not run this race, you can always find another marathon over the next couple of weeks to enter and show off all of your training and hard work.

Avoid second-guessing what could go wrong on race day, approach it with a relaxed and open state of mind and 'go with the flow'.

94. Count!

1 mile done...that's $1/26^{th}$ ... 13 miles done, I'm halfway!

Breaking down the distance and checking off the miles is a great distraction and gives motivation while you are running.

If you want to, you can covert the miles into kilometres, they count down much faster than the miles - which feels awesome!

Find creative ways to count down and put the miles into perspective.

3 miles to go - that's less than a Parkrun!
10km to go, that's my easy recovery run distance.

95. Arrange A Rendezvous

Pre-plan where family and friends will stand to cheer you on. You will look forward to it!

The crowds along a marathon can be huge, up to ten or twelve people deep. Pre-arrange with your supporters where they will stand to cheer you on. You can look forward to seeing them and know exactly where to spot them when you get close.

Expecting to see friends and family but not knowing whereabouts along the 26.2-mile course they will be can be frustrating, distracting and disheartening. Make sure you know roughly where they are. If they can run to an additional spot to cheer you on, then that is an added bonus for you too.

96. Grunt, Nod or Say 'Hi'

If you are stood on the start line with over a thousand other runners, don't be afraid to say 'hi' to the person standing next to you. The running community is fantastic, encouraging and welcoming.

Caution, however, to listening to someone panicking on the start-line, know whether this could affect your own confidence. If it might put doubts in your mind, then excuse yourself away, if you are confident, then offer them some support and a friendly smile.

Acknowledging other runners during the marathon will also help you, give a 'well done' as you pass someone, say 'thanks' to someone passing you and giving you encouragement.

The last few miles of a marathon can feel quite lonely if you are starting to feel tired, having some support can be essential, don't shy away from it.

If someone wants to run next to you and follow your pace then try not to get annoyed, take it as a compliment that they think you are running strongly.

Beware of being that annoying chatty person! Gauge whether your new running buddy really wants a full-blown conversation, ask if you can chat.

You might just like to run next to someone for support but in silence. This is a good thing! Get strength from them being with you. If they speed up, don't feel pressured to speed up with them, stick to your plan.

97. Speed Up Towards The Finish

You are going to make it, the end is in sight!

Unless you have forgotten to take your nutrition, it is likely that you will have a little bit of energy left for a speedy finish!

You might have found the last 4 miles hard going, but that last mile is often the fastest mile for many marathon runners.

Your adrenaline will surge, the crowds will roar, you will feel emotional, you will feel elated and your legs will start to move faster!

Use up your last reserves of energy by having the most fantastic finish!

98. Hands Off of Your Watch

Don't stop your watch on the finish line.

You have worked hard, for months, to cross this finish line. You deserve a fantastic finishers photo that you can hang up on your wall with pride. Do not ruin it by looking down to stop your watch on the line.

The event will have timed your marathon for you, your result will be official and published, to there really is no need to stop your watch the moment you cross the line. Look ahead, smile and take in the pleasure of finishing your marathon!

You can stop your watch 30 seconds later, it's ok.

If you are obsessed with Strava, then you can always crop the extra time off of it later.

99. Have A Finish Line Bag Prepared

Include some warm, clean kit and some food in your bag at the finish.

You are likely to get very cold, very quickly once you have finished your marathon. Ensure you have some dry and warm clothes available to put straight on. Most marathons have a bag drop, so you can leave a rucksack safely to collect at the end.

Have some recovery food and a drink in your bag.

You will be grateful for your own pre-planning when you get there.

100. Take Time Off

You do not need to stop running completely after Race Day. Aim to have some unscheduled, relaxed, fun runs with no agenda.

Try not to rush back into training, let your body and your mind recover.

RACE REPORTS

101. What To Do When You Have Finished Your Marathon...

Write a race report within a day or two of your race. A race report is the best way to record everything that happened and to help you to learn from your mistakes or remember the actions that helped to make your race a success.

Record your actions in the build-up to the race, what you ate, how you felt, what your thoughts were at the start line, did you go off too fast? Why? Funny or interesting things you remember seeing or thinking during the race when you ate or drank in the race. How the last miles felt. How crossing the finishing line felt. How was recovery? This will help you to identify things you could do better next time, if anything went wrong then why and also which bits worked really well for you and that you should repeat for next time.

Always keep a note of your race times, you will be amazed at how much progress you make each year.

Many marathons now offer on-site medal engraving where they add your time to the back of the medal. This is a fantastic way of keeping track.

Plan your next race!

After writing your race report, I bet you are thinking that you could have done something differently....book your next race in straight away and ride the momentum.

Make sure you leave yourself a few weeks to recover before you start properly training again. Recovery is key, both mentally and physically. When booking your next race consider your recovery time and factor in time to start training again...don't book in for next weekend!

Share your Race Report with pride and tell EVERYONE that you have run a marathon!

Be proud! You are in the minority of people who have been bold enough to take on the challenge of running a marathon.

It doesn't matter if you walked a bit, or even if you crawled across that finish line. You did it. Be proud, tell everyone, remind yourself of how awesome you are. Most importantly, book in the next one!

Printed in Great Britain
by Amazon